american|GOVERNMENT

Lynn Garland

Student Activity Manual

bju **press**®

Greenville, South Carolina

NOTE:
The fact that materials produced by other publishers may be referred to in this volume does not constitute an endorsement of the content or theological position of materials produced by such publishers. Any references and ancillary materials are listed as an aid to the student or the teacher and in an attempt to maintain the accepted academic standards of the publishing industry.

American Government Student Activity Manual

For use with **American Government, Second Edition**

Lynn Garland

Compositor	**Cover**	**Design**	**Project Editor**
Carol Ingalls	John Bjerk	Duane Nichols	Manda Kalagayan

Produced in cooperation with the Bob Jones University Department of History of the College of Arts and Science, the School of Religion, and Bob Jones Academy.

Cover Photo
The White House

© 2004 BJU Press
Greenville, South Carolina 29614

Printed in the United States of America
All rights reserved

ISBN 978-1-57924-687-7

15 14 13 12 11 10 9 8 7 6 5 4 3

Contents

UNIT IV: THE LEGISLATIVE BRANCH

UNIT V: THE EXECUTIVE BRANCH

Chapter 16: Foreign Policy

UNIT VI: THE JUDICIAL BRANCH

Chapter 17: The Judiciary

Chapter 18: Civil Rights and Civil Responsibilities

Breaking God's Laws
Answer the questions after reading the following Scripture passages.

II Kings 11—
1. How did Athaliah break God's laws, and why did she do this? _____
_____

2. How did Athaliah's subjects respond to her sin? _____
_____
_____
_____

3. How did God respond to Athaliah's sin? _____
_____

II Chronicles 26:14–20—
1. How did Uzziah break God's laws, and why did he do this? _____
_____
_____

2. How did the priests respond to Uzziah's sin? _____
_____

3. How did God respond to Uzziah's sin? _____
_____

Discussion—
1. What is God's response to subjects who remove a ruler who has broken God's laws? _____
_____
_____
_____

2. Using II Chronicles 26:14–16, discuss how this passage illustrates that there is a proper
separation of church and state even in a theocracy. _____
_____
_____
_____
_____

Paul's Example

Throughout the book of Acts, Paul's knowledge and understanding of government are illustrated. Read the following passages and answer the questions.

Acts 16:16–39—
   1. What information gives insight into Paul's knowledge of Roman law? _____
   _____
   _____

   2. How did Paul and Silas respond to this unlawful situation? _____
   _____
   _____

   3. How did Paul make the government officials accountable for their actions?
   _____

Acts 23:1–10—
   1. What did the high priest command be done to Paul and why? _____
   _____
   _____

   2. What two religious/political groups were in attendance? _____

   3. What observations can be made concerning Paul in this passage? _____
   _____
   _____

Acts 25:1–12—
   1. How did Paul answer the Jews from Jerusalem while appealing his case before Festus?
   _____
   _____

   2. As a Roman, to whom was Paul's final appeal? _____

Discuss how Paul's example applies to Christians today.

_____
_____
_____
_____
_____

Do You Remember?

Answer the following questions.

1. Define *government.* _____

2. Why is government a necessary part of this world? _____
   _____
   _____

3. What does God call governments to do? _____
   _____

4. Identify the type of government that is ruled directly by God or the clergy. _____

5. Define *patriotism.* _____
   _____

6. What is meant when we say that mankind was made in the image of God? _____
   _____
   _____

7. What is the absence of any government called? _____

8. Define *righteousness* according to law and morality. _____
   _____

9. What two activities allow the believer to press for government change? _____
   _____

10. What is *jingoism?* _____

11. List the qualities that God invested mankind with that reflect His character. _____
    _____
    _____

12. Define *human depravity.* _____
    _____
    _____

13. How does good government prove itself to be good? _____
    _____
    _____

14. In what context does Scripture establish submission and obedience to government?
    _____
    _____
    _____

15. Explain the creation mandate. _____

_____

_____

_____

_____

16. How is mankind unique? _____

_____

_____

17. What is one of the most condemning truths concerning the human race?

_____

_____

_____

18. What is the only way for a government to be truly just? _____

_____

_____

19. What attitudes are Christian citizens to have toward government? _____

_____

_____

20. From where did David's attitude of respect for civil authority come? _____

_____

21. What two ungodly governments did Paul face? _____

_____

22. Who two things are necessary if Christians are to participate effectively in government?

_____

_____

_____

23. Discuss the Trinity and the hierarchy of authority. _____

_____

_____

_____

_____

24. Did God intend that every human fulfill the creation mandate in the same capacity? Explain
your answer. _____

_____

_____

_____

Mayflower Compact, 1620

The Mayflower Compact was the first document establishing a form of government in colonial America. Read it and the excerpt from William Bradford's *Of Plymouth Plantation*. The excerpt gives the circumstances surrounding the writing and signing of the Mayflower Compact.

Mayflower Compact

In the name of God, Amen. We, whose names are underwritten, the loyal subjects of our dread sovereigne Lord, King James, by the grace of God, of Great Britaine, France, and Ireland king, defender of the faith, etc., having undertaken, for the glory of God, and advancement of the Christian faith, and honour of our king and country, a voyage to plant the first colony in the Northerne parts of Virginia, doe, by these presents solemnly and mutually in the presence of God, and one of another, covenant and combine ourselves together into a civill body politick, for our better ordering and preservation and furtherance of the ends aforesaid; and by virtue hereof to enacte, constitute, and frame such just and equall laws, ordinances, acts, constitutions, and offices, from time to time, as shall be thought most meete and convenient for the generall good of the Colonie unto which we promise all due submission and obedience. In witness whereof we have hereunder subscribed our names at Cap-Codd the 11 of November, in the year of the raigne of our sovereigne lord, King James, of England, France, and Ireland, the eighteenth, and of Scotland the fifte-fourth. Anno. Dom. 1620.

Of Plymouth Plantation

I shall a little return back, and begin with a combination made by them before they came ashore; being the first foundation of their government in this place. Occasioned partly by the discontented and mutinous speeches that some of the strangers amongst them had let fall from them in the ship: That when they came ashore they would use their own liberty, for none had power to command them, the patent they had being for Virginia and not for New England, which belonged to another government, with which the Virginia Company had nothing to do. And partly that such an act by them done, this their condition considered, might be as firm as any patent, and in some respects more sure. (Chapter XI)

(taken from William Bradford, Of Plymouth Plantation, ed. Samuel Eliot Morison. New York: Knopf, 1952.)

Explain the meaning of the following phrases from the Mayflower Compact.

1. "covenant and combine ourselves together into a civill body politick" _____

_____

2. "for our better ordering and preservation" _____

_____

3. "by virtue hereof to enacte, constitute, and frame such just and equall laws, ordinances, acts,

constitutions, and offices" _____

_____

4. "from time to time, as shall be thought most meete and convenient for the generall good of the Colonie" _____

    _____

    _____

5. "unto which we promise all due submission and obedience" _____

    _____

    _____

Using the excerpt from *Of Plymouth Plantation* and other sources, list the reasons the Mayflower Compact was written.

_____

_____

_____

_____

_____

_____

_____

Discussion—When the colonists wrote the Mayflower Compact and promised to obey it, were they establishing a separate government from England? Support your answer.

_____

_____

_____

_____

_____

_____

Christianity's Influence

Answer the following questions.

1. Who was called the "old doctor" by a famous student?_____

2. What event transformed lives, influenced society, and shaped the generation whose ideas and arms gave birth to our republic?_____

3. What began to replace faith in the last quarter of the seventeenth century?_____

    _____

4. What pastor attained the rank of major general and served under George Washington during the War for Independence?_____

5. Where did George Whitefield place much of the blame for the general spiritual decline in the colonies?_____

6. In what three areas of American society did the Great Awakening bring notable changes?

    _____

7. Which college was opened as a Christian school for Indians in 1754?_____

8. Where and under whose ministry did the revival fires begin to flicker in 1734?

    _____

9. Which religious group was given privileged status by the Quebec Act of 1774?

    _____

10. Who was the only minister to sign the Declaration of Independence?_____

11. What form of government was designed at the Constitutional Convention to restrain tyranny?

    _____

    _____

12. Which founding father's political thought was greatly shaped by John Witherspoon?

    _____

13. How was the church important to the War for Independence? _____

    _____

14. During the eighteenth century, who was usually the best-educated man and most influential leader in the community? _____

15. How were the actions of the British Parliament from 1765 to 1775 harmful to the colonies?

    _____

People, Documents, and Events

Place the following people, documents, and events in the correct chronological order in the chart below. Include a date for each and explain its colonial importance.

Quebec Act, Mayflower Compact, Martin Luther, "Old Deluder Satan" Act, Fundamental Orders of Connecticut, Great Awakening, John Witherspoon, Act of 1642

PEOPLE, DOCUMENTS, EVENTS	TIME PERIOD	COLONIAL IMPORTANCE

 Name _____

Systems of Government

What are the three major government systems? Define and give an example of each.

1. _____

_____

_____

_____

2. _____

_____

_____

_____

3. _____

_____

_____

_____

Identify whether each of the following statements is describing a unitary, federal, or confederate government.

_____ 1. The national government has few or no powers.

_____ 2. The government's power resides in the central government.

_____ 3. The Articles of Confederation established this type of government in early American history.

_____ 4. A nation's power is divided among national, regional, and local governments.

_____ 5. Local units are created by the central government to help administer governments.

_____ 6. This government guards against tyranny through the separation of its government powers.

_____ 7. The European Union is an example of this government type.

_____ 8. Israel and Japan are examples of this government type.

_____ 9. This type of government works well in large countries made up of people with different needs and goals.

_____ 10. Brazil and India are examples of this government type.

Using additional resources, identify whether the following countries elect their executive through a presidential or parliamentary system.

_____ 1. Bolivia

_____ 2. Czech Republic

_____ 3. Fiji Islands

_____ 4. Guyana

_____ 5. Mexico

_____ 6. Switzerland

_____ 7. Taiwan

_____ 8. Turkey

_____ 9. Uzbekistan

_____ 10. Zimbabwe

What About Your State?

Answer the following questions concerning your state and local governments.

Legislative Branch

1. Is your state's legislature bicameral or unicameral?_____
_____

2. If your state is bicameral, what are the names of the two houses?_____
_____

3. How many senators and house members does your state have?_____
_____

Executive Branch

1. Are your governor and lieutenant governor elected together or separately?_____
_____
_____

2. Who are your state's governor and lieutenant governor?_____
_____
_____

3. What state executive offices are elected by popular vote? Who is serving in these offices?
_____
_____
_____
_____

4. Which of your state's executive offices are appointed by the governor?_____
_____

Judicial Branch

1. Are your state's supreme court judges elected or appointed?_____
2. List your state's supreme court judges and chief justice._____
_____
_____
_____
_____
_____

Local Government

1. Which county officials are elected by the voters, and who is serving in these offices?

   _____

   _____

   _____

   _____

   _____

2. What town officials are elected, and who is serving in these offices?

   _____

   _____

   _____

   _____

   _____

Reviewing Forms of Government

Answer the following questions.

1. Why does the Constitution limit states' powers? _____

_____

2. According to the Constitution, which powers do the states retain? _____

_____

3. Besides the Constitution, what limits a state's power? _____

4. What are powers given to the national government by the Constitution which define the of its

limits authority? _____

5. What did the states create to assist in administering their laws and policies? _____

_____

6. What gives a city its name and serves as its constitution? _____

7. What are special districts? _____

_____

_____

8. Who is the chief officer of a state's executive branch? _____

9. What is the heart of American government? _____

10. What are the three branches of national government? _____

_____

11. How is Congress divided? _____

12. Who is the chief executive officer of the executive branch of government? _____

13. Which branch of government interprets the laws? _____

14. What does *incorporation* mean? _____

_____

_____

15. What is an urban, local system of government that includes cities, villages, and towns?

_____

16. Which state does not have a bicameral legislature? _____

17. What is the political division within a county? _____

18. What does the Constitution establish as the highest court in the land? _____

19. Define *direct democracy*. _____

_____

_____

20. What is the absence of government? _____

21. Define *republic*. _____

    _____

    _____

22. Identify the system in which the people directly elect the president independently of the legislative branch. _____

23. Explain the unitary system of government. _____

    _____

    _____

    _____

24. Define *indirect democracy*. _____

    _____

    _____

25. In which system of government are the legislative and executive branches inseparably linked?

    _____

26. In which system of government does an elite group rule? _____

27. What has control over the creation and existence of cities within a state? _____

    _____

14

Impact of the English Bill of Rights

Using the information on pages 48–49 in the text, identify specific provisions in the English Bill of Rights that are reflected in the following provisions of the U.S. Bill of Rights.

U.S. BILL OF RIGHTS   1689 ENGLISH BILL OF RIGHTS

1. Freedoms of Religion, of
   the Press, and to Petition
   _____
   _____
   _____
   _____

2. The Right to Bear Arms
   _____
   _____
   _____

3. Rights of the Accused in
   Criminal Trials
   _____
   _____
   _____

4. Rights of Citizens in Civil
   Trials
   _____
   _____
   _____

5. Cruel, Unusual, and
   Unjust Punishments
   _____
   _____
   _____

6. Unspecified Rights
   _____
   _____

Discussion

Why were only Protestant subjects allowed to have arms for defense in the seventh right of the

English Bill of Rights? _____

_____

_____

_____

 *Name* _____

Chapter 4   Activity 2

Democracy's Milestones

Place the following democratic milestones in chronological order with the date in which they occurred. You may need to consult outside sources for some of the dates.

MILESTONES	CHRONOLOGICAL ORDER
Magna Carta	_____
Decline of the Roman Republic and the rise of the Roman Empire	_____
U.S. Constitution ratification completed	_____
Roman Republic emerged	_____
Roman Twelve Tables	_____
Athenian democracy established	_____
English Bill of Rights	_____
	_____

Answer the following questions.

1. What did our founders fear that pure democracy would lead to? _____

   _____

2. What are the two Greek words that combine to form the word *democracy*, and what do they

   mean? _____

   _____

3. What is federalism? _____

   _____

4. What was the primary responsibility of tribunes in the Roman Republic? _____

   _____

   _____

5. What is due process? _____

   _____

   _____

6. What were the two major issues that confronted the Constitutional framers? _____

   _____

   _____

   _____

   _____

Electoral Systems

Using other resources, determine the electoral system (proportional or majority-plurality) of the following countries and describe each country's governing body. (Majority-plurality = single-seat constituencies) Austria is filled in for you.

COUNTRY	SYSTEM TYPE	GOVERNING BODY DESCRIPTION
Austria	Proportional Representation	Parliament: Two chambers National Council—elected by proportional representation; Federal Council—elected by provisional parliaments
Bolivia		
Canada		
Georgia		
Israel		
Japan		
Kenya		
Peru		
Sweden		
Zambia		

Understanding Democracy

Answer completely.

1. How does moral responsibility strengthen democracy? _____
   _____
   _____
   _____

2. Why did the English Bill of Rights mark the beginning of a democratic government in
   England? _____
   _____
   _____
   _____

3. List and explain the five characteristics of democratic government. _____
   _____
   _____
   _____
   _____
   _____
   _____
   _____
   _____
   _____
   _____

4. What conditions must be present for a democracy to develop and be successful?
   _____
   _____
   _____

5. How does the Constitution limit government? _____
   _____
   _____
   _____

6. What did the founders recognize as the reason that a direct democracy tends toward mob
   rule?_____

 Name _____

Declaration and Resolves

The First Continental Congress, in defense of their rights as British subjects, compiled a list of grievances to be sent to George III. Read the following excerpts from the Declaration and Resolves. Using the excerpts and other sources, answer the following questions.

Whereas, since the close of the last war, the British parliament, claiming a power, of right, to bind the people of America by statutes in all cases whatsoever, hath, in some acts, expressly imposed taxes on them, and in others, under various pretences, but in fact for the purpose of raising a revenue, hath imposed rates and duties payable in these colonies, established a board of commissioners, with unconstitutional powers, and extended the jurisdiction of courts of admiralty, not only for collecting the said duties, but for the trial of causes merely arising within the body of a country:

And whereas, in consequence of other statutes, judges, who before held only estates at will in their offices, have been made dependent on the crown alone for their salaries, and standing armies kept in times of peace: And whereas it has lately been resolved in parliament, that by force of a statute, made in the thirty-fifth year of the reign of King Henry the Eighth, colonists may be transported to England, and tried there upon accusations for treasons and misprisions, or concealments of treasons committed in the colonies, and by a late statute, such trials have been directed in cases therein mentioned:

And whereas, assemblies have been frequently dissolved, contrary to the rights of the people, when they attempted to deliberate on grievances; and their dutiful, humble, loyal, and reasonable petitions to the crown for redress, have been repeatedly treated with contempt, by his Majesty's ministers of state:

1. When did the Continental Congress say that the British Parliament had begun to "bind the people of America by statutes?" _____

_____

2. For what purpose did Parliament impose rates and duties? _____

3. What did Parliament establish that had unconstitutional powers? _____

4. How was the jurisdiction of the Courts of Admiralty extended? _____

_____

_____

5. How had Parliament changed the method of paying judges? Why could this prove to be a problem? _____

_____

6. Why was keeping a standing army during times of peace a grievance? _____

_____

_____

_____

7. What statute had Parliament enforced that made it legal to transport colonists for trial in England? Why was this a grievance? _____

_____

_____

_____

8. For what crimes could colonists be tried in England? _____

_____

9. How had the king's ministers of state treated the colonists? _____

_____

_____

From the following list of Declaration and Resolves signers, choose an individual, briefly research his life, and write a brief paragraph on the most interesting facts about him.

COLONIES	SIGNERS
New Hampshire	John Sullivan and Nathaniel Folsom
Massachusetts	Thomas Cushing and Robert Treat Paine
Rhode Island	Stephen Hopkins and Samuel Ward
Connecticut	Eliphalet Dyer and Roger Sherman
New York	John Alsop and Isaac Low
Pennsylvania	John Morton and Edward Biddle
New Jersey	Stephen Crane and William Livingston
Delaware	Caesar Rodney and Thomas McKeane
Maryland	William Pace and Samuel Chase
Virginia	Richard Henry Lee and Benjamin Harrison
North Carolina	Joseph Hawes and Richard Caswell
South Carolina	Henry Middleton and Thomas Lynch

_____

_____

_____

_____

_____

_____

 Name _____

Scripture and Government

Different aspects of government are referenced in Scripture. Read the following passages and briefly explain what is being stated concerning government.

1. Exodus 18:25–26—_____

_____

_____

_____

_____

2. Deuteronomy 1:3, 13—_____

_____

_____

_____

_____

3. Deuteronomy 1:17—_____

_____

_____

_____

_____

4. Deuteronomy 16:19—_____

_____

_____

_____

_____

5. Deuteronomy 17:15—_____

_____

6. Deuteronomy 17:16–19—_____

_____

_____

_____

_____

7. Matthew 20:27—_____

_____

Movements Toward Independence

Complete the chart using the textbook.

Event	Description	Results
Glorious Revolution		
French & Indian War		
George III Becomes King		
1765 Stamp Act		
Boston Massacre		
Boston Tea Party		
First Continental Congress		
Battles of Lexington & Concord		
Second Continental Congress		

"Compact Together"

In the days prior to the Constitutional Convention, Elizur Goodrich preached the sermon "The Principles of Civil Union and Happiness Considered and Recommended" to the governor and legislature of Connecticut. Pastor Goodrich began the sermon with a description of Jerusalem and referenced Psalm 122:3, "Jerusalem is builded as a city that is compact together." Throughout the sermon, Goodrich highlighted the qualities of a happy, strong Jerusalem and encouraged those present to incorporate these qualities into the new American government.

Using a Matthew Henry commentary, explain the meaning of Psalm 122:3.

_____

_____

_____

_____

Read the following excerpts from the sermon reprinted from *Political Sermons of the American Founding Era (1730–1805)*, ed. Ellis Sandoz, (Indianapolis: LibertyPress, 1991).

Jerusalem was a city, defended with strong walls, the metropolis of the kingdom of Israel. . . . Its inhabitants were not a loose, disconnected people, but most strictly united, not only among themselves, but with all the tribes of Israel, into a holy nation and commonwealth, under Jehovah their king and their God. . . . Hence both by divine appointment, and the common consent of the nation, it was established as the local centre of communion in all the privileges of their civil and sacred constitution. There were the thrones of judgement, . . . the supreme courts of justice, and of the public administration. . . .

In all these respects, whether Jerusalem be considered in a natural, civil or religious view, its strength and beauty consisted in being builded "as a city, that is compact together." . . . Religion therefore, and public spirit were united in the ardent affection of the pious Israelites, toward Jerusalem, which they preferred above their chief joy.

We have also a Jerusalem, adorned with brighter glories. . . . We enjoy all the privileges of a free government, the blessings of the gospel of peace. . . . This is our Jerusalem.

The principles of society are the laws, which Almighty God has established in the moral world, . . . which direct mankind to the highest perfection, and supreme happiness of their nature. They are fixed and unchangeable. . . .

But to close this discourse and address; . . . Encourage your rulers in building up our Jerusalem, on the strong foundations of truth and righteousness—maintain in your hearts conduct, those principles and maxims of love, benevolence and goodness, which will render you a united, happy, and prosperous people. Let God be honoured, and the grace of the Redeemer exalted; the sabbath sanctified; the worship and ordinances of the Lord's house maintained: the pious and virtuous education of the rising generation, religiously regarded; and a firm inviolable adherence to the laws and institutions of Christ, manifested by all orders and ranks of men. Then virtue and peace, righteousness, mercy and the fear of God, will flourish; and every member of the community will be found fixed in his proper place, and discharging the duties of it.

Answer the following questions in light of Psalm 122:3, the sermon excerpts, and the time period in which the Constitution was written.

1. Why do you think Pastor Goodrich chose Psalm 122:3 as the key verse in his sermon?

   _____

   _____

   _____

   _____

   _____

2. List the qualities possessed by Jerusalem. _____

   _____

   _____

   _____

   _____

   _____

3. What did Pastor Goodrich state "our Jerusalem" enjoyed? _____

   _____

4. What did the Almighty God establish in the moral world and for what purpose? _____

   _____

   _____

5. With what admonitions does Pastor Goodrich close his sermon? _____

   _____

   _____

   _____

   _____

   _____

6. What does Pastor Goodrich say will result if the leadership follows his admonitions?

   _____

   _____

7. In your opinion, could a secular government established on these biblical principles produce the society Pastor Goodrich highlighted? Support your answer.

   _____

   _____

   _____

   _____

   _____

Do You Remember?

Answer the following questions.

1. At which assembly was the Declaration of Independence created? _____
   _____

2. What law did the 1765 Stamp Act violate? _____

3. How did Great Britain influence American colonial government? _____
   _____

4. Which Enlightenment philosopher's writings on government influenced America's founding
   fathers? _____

5. Which assembly was convened on May 25, 1787, what was its purpose, and who was chosen
   president? _____
   _____

6. What is a boycott, and why did the colonists institute one? _____
   _____
   _____

7. What did the Declaration of Independence reflect? _____
   _____

8. What did the Virginia Plan advocate, and whom did it favor? _____
   _____
   _____
   _____
   _____

9. How was Washington's inauguration both an end and a beginning? _____
   _____

10. What catalytic events shook colonial America and encouraged independence? _____
    _____
    _____
    _____

11. What is deism, and out of what did it grow? _____
    _____
    _____

12. What did the Second Continental Congress set out to do, and what was the result? _____
    _____
    _____

13. What did the New Jersey Plan advocate, and whom did it favor? _____

_____

_____

14. What issues confronted the Constitutional Convention? _____

_____

_____

15. Who were the Federalists and Anti-Federalists? In which states did these two groups have the toughest battles? What was added to the Constitution as a result of Anti-Federalist demands?

_____

_____

_____

16. Which assembly issued a Declaration of Grievances to King George III? _____

_____

17. What were the four major truths Jefferson presented in the Declaration of Independence?

_____

_____

_____

_____

18. Why were the Articles of Confederation so difficult to get ratified? _____

_____

19. What two events showed the states that their national union under the Articles of Confederation needed to be redefined, and how did these events illustrate this need?

_____

_____

_____

_____

20. What was the Three-Fifths Compromise, and which specific part of government was directly affected? _____

_____

_____

21. What was the Connecticut Compromise, or Great Compromise? _____

_____

_____

22. What two procedural rules were adopted at the beginning of the Constitutional Convention? Why were they important? _____

_____

_____

_____

 american|GOVERNMENT *Name* _____

Chapter 6   Activity 1

Strict or Broad?

Read the following quotations from justices and judges. Identify whether the quote indicates the judge or justice may be a strict or broad constitutional constructionist and explain your answer.

1. Robert Bork—"There is no other sense in which the Constitution can be what article VI proclaims it to be: 'Law. . . .' This means, of course, that a judge, no matter on what court he sits, may never create new constitutional rights or destroy old ones. Any time he does so, he violates not only the limits to his own authority but, and for that reason, also violates the rights of the legislature and the people. . . . [T]he philosophy of original understanding is thus a necessary inference from the structure of government apparent on the face of the Constitution."

   _____

   _____

   _____

2. William J. Brennan, Jr.—"This Court inescapably has the duty, as the ultimate arbiter of the meaning of our Constitution, to say whether, when individuals condemned to death stand before our bar, 'moral concepts' require us to hold that the law has progressed to the point where we should declare that the punishment of death, like punishments on the rack, the screw and the wheel, is no longer morally tolerable in our society."

   _____

   _____

   _____

3. Hugo L. Black—"Our Constitution was not written in the sands to be washed away by each wave of new judges blown in by each successive political wind."

   _____

   _____

   _____

4. Warren E. Burger—"Judges rule on the basis of law, not public opinion, and they should be totally indifferent to pressures of the times."

   _____

   _____

   _____

5. William O. Douglas—"We deal with a right of privacy older than the Bill of Rights—older than our political parties, older than our school system."

   _____

   _____

   _____

Popular Sovereignty

The following excerpt on popular sovereignty is from Alexis de Tocqueville's *Democracy in America*. Read this selection and discuss Tocqueville's thoughts on America's popular sovereignty before, during, and after the Revolution.

I have already observed that, from their origin, the sovereignty of the people was the fundamental principle of most of the British colonies in America. It was far, however, from then exercising as much influence on the government of society as it now does. . . . It could not ostensibly disclose itself in the laws of the colonies which were still forced to obey the mother country; it was there obliged to rule secretly in the provincial assemblies, and especially in the townships. . . . American society at that time was not yet prepared to adopt it with all its consequences. Intelligence in New England and wealth in the country south of the Hudson . . . long exercised a sort of aristocratic influence, which tended to keep the exercise of social power in the hands of a few. Not all the public functionaries were chosen by popular vote, nor were all the citizens voters. The electoral franchise was everywhere somewhat restricted and made dependent on a certain qualification, which was very low in the North and more considerable in the South. . . . The American Revolution broke out, and the doctrine of the sovereignty of the people came out of the townships and took possession of the state. Every class was enlisted in its cause; battles were fought and victories obtained for it; it became the law of laws. . . . At the present day . . . [s]ometimes the laws are made by the people in a body, as in Athens; and sometimes its representatives, chosen by universal suffrage, transact business in its name and under its immediate supervision. . . . The people reign in the American political world as the Deity does in the universe. They are the cause and the aim of all things; everything comes from them, and everything is absorbed in them.

Discussion

_____

_____

_____

_____

_____

_____

_____

_____

_____

Constitutional Familiarity

Find the following lines in the Constitution and record a short summary of each.

1. Article I, Section 3, Clause 5 _____

_____

2. Article II, Section 1, Clause 7 _____

3. Article IV, Section 3, Clause 1 _____

4. Article II, Section 1, Clause 4 _____

5. Article III, Section 3, Clause 1 _____

6. Amendment XXVII _____

7. Article I, Section 8, Clause 5 _____

_____

_____

8. Amendment XXII, Section 1 _____

9. Article II, Section 2, Clause 1 _____

_____

_____

10. Article I, Section 2, Clause 2 _____

11. Article V _____

12. Amendment XXV, Section 1 _____

_____

13. Article I, Section 3, Clause 3 _____

14. Article II, Section 1, Clause 2 _____

15. Article I, Section 8, Clause 11 _____

16. Article III, Section 1 _____

_____

17. Amendment XVII _____

18. Article I, Section 2, Clause 5 _____

_____

19. Article I, Section 3, Clause 6 _____

20. Amendment XXV, Section 3 _____

_____

_____

Where are each of the following located in the Constitution?

1. When Congress shall assemble each year _____

2. "We the people of the United States" _____

3. The Senate is to be composed of two senators from each state. _____

4. Congress determines the time for the president's election. _____

5. The trial of all crimes except impeachment shall be by jury. _____

6. The president is to give Congress a State of the Union message. _____

7. House members are to serve two-year terms. _____

8. Each state is to have a republican form of government. _____

9. Congress has the power to tax incomes. _____

10. All bills dealing with taxation must start in the House of Representatives.

    _____

11. Only with permission from Congress may U.S. citizens accept titles or honors from foreign countries. _____

12. The terms of senators and representatives end at noon on the third of January and their successors' terms begin. _____

In Review

Identify the term or terms each of the following statements defines.

1. Branch whose function is to interpret the law _____

2. Was added by the Constitutional framers so that future Congresses would have the authority to meet future needs _____

3. The first ten amendments added to the Constitution _____

4. Principle that prohibits government from having absolute power _____

5. A situation created when one branch of the government brings the political process to a halt

   _____

6. Introduces the Constitution by explaining its nature and purpose _____

7. The right to send official mail free of charge _____

8. Grants of money allocated by Congress to finance government programs _____

9. The group, composed of electors from each state, that elects the president _____

10. A court's power to hear a case before it is considered by any other court _____

    _____

11. Constitutional provision that upholds the United States Constitution as the highest law of the nation _____

12. Defaming a person in writing _____

13. Five instruments used to keep racial minorities from voting or to lessen their vote

    _____

    _____

    _____

    _____

    _____

14. Enacted by several states following the Civil War as a means of keeping poor blacks from voting _____

15. Those who take a broader, more creative approach to constitutional interpretation

    _____

16. The formal introduction of an amendment _____

17. The formal approval process of an amendment _____

18. Two principles that limit government _____

19. The power of the judicial branch to review the constitutionality of laws passed by the legislative branch _____

20. Branch whose primary function is to make laws _____

21. The minimum number needed to transact business _____

22. The journal or record of what each house of Congress does daily _____

_____

23. The process by which a foreign-born person gains citizenship _____

24. Court order forcing authorities to quickly charge and try an arrested person or release him

_____

25. Branch whose primary function is to carry out the nation's laws _____

26. The complete forgiveness of a crime and its consequent punishment _____

27. A court's power to decide appeals _____

28. Legal process of returning a fugitive to the state in which he has been charged with a crime

_____

29. Defaming a person verbally _____

30. Money deposited to guarantee a court appearance, allowing the accused freedom while awaiting trial _____

31. Two terms for the right to vote _____

32. Those who believe that the text of the Constitution is important and that any interpretation should be kept to a minimum _____

33. A more formal means of adapting the Constitution to change _____

34. Principle of separating powers among different branches of government to prevent any group or individual from gaining too much control _____

35. The process of bringing up the president or other government officials on criminal charges

_____

36. The division of power between national and state levels of government _____

37. Principle that makes the people the ultimate source of their government's authority

_____

38. A two-house legislative system _____

39. Leader elected by the Senate who serves as leader of the Senate when the vice president is absent _____

40. An official in both houses who is responsible to bring in members who are absent and needed for a quorum _____

41. Automatic veto of a bill the president leaves unsigned for ten days during a congressional adjournment _____

42. Bill permitting punishment without trial _____

43. The temporary postponement of punishment _____

44. Laws passed and applied to actions that were not criminal when they were committed

_____

45. A document requiring a person to appear in court as a witness _____

46. An official who is still in office but has not been reelected _____

47. A panel of citizens who consider the prosecution's case against the accused to determine whether there is enough evidence to go to trial _____

48. Case in which Chief Justice John Marshall established the principle of judicial review

_____

49. The modern militia under the control of the army and air force _____

50. Certain legal procedures by which the government must abide in order to protect the rights of the accused _____

51. Drawing district lines so that black districts' votes have less impact _____

52. Principle that keeps each branch of government in check through the power of another branch of government _____

53. A counting of the population every ten years to determine state representation branch_____

54. Allowed previous voters and their relatives to vote without facing a literacy test or other requirements _____

55. The president's power to refuse to sign a bill into law _____

Answer the following questions.

1. What is the structure of the U.S. Constitution?

_____

_____

_____

2. What are the six purposes of the Constitution according to the Preamble?

_____

_____

_____

_____

_____

_____

3. What are the six basic principles found in the Constitution?

_____

_____

_____

_____

_____

_____

4. What are the three things the federal government must guarantee to all
   the states?

_____

_____

_____

Citizens Then

Tocqueville, in his discussion on the federal Constitution in *Democracy in America,* makes some observations concerning federalism and American citizens. Read the excerpt and answer the following questions.

In examining the Constitution of the United States, which is the most perfect constitution that ever existed, one is startled at the variety of information and the excellence of discernment that it presupposes in the people whom it is meant to govern. . . . When once the general theory is comprehended, many difficulties remain to be solved in its application. . . . The whole structure of the government is artificial and conventional, and it would be ill adapted to a people which has not been long accustomed to conduct its own affairs, or to one in which the science of politics has not descended to the humblest classes of society. . . . I scarcely ever met with a plain American citizen who could not distinguish, with surprising facility, the obligations created by the laws of Congress from those created by the laws of his own State, and who, after having discriminated between the matters which come under the cognizance of the Union and those which the local legislature is competent to regulate, could not point out the exact limit of the separate jurisdictions of the Federal courts and the tribunals of the State.

1. What characteristic does Tocqueville say the Constitution presupposes about the people it is meant to govern? Could Tocqueville make the same observation about today's average American citizen? Explain your answer.

_____

_____

_____

_____

_____

2. To which two groups of people does Tocqueville say American federalism would be ill adapted? Explain why he would single out these two groups?

_____

_____

_____

_____

3. What observations does Tocqueville make about "a plain American citizen"? Could he say the same about today's plain American citizen? Explain your answer.

_____

_____

_____

_____

Your State Constitution

Locate a copy of your state constitution. Answer the following questions.

1. When was your state constitution adopted? _____

2. Does your state constitution have a preamble, or a declaration of rights, or both? List the
   stated rights. _____

   _____

   _____

3. List the constitution's articles and their titles and amendments (if any).

   _____

   _____

   _____

   _____

   _____

   _____

   _____

   _____

   _____

   _____

   _____

   _____

   _____

   _____

   _____

   _____

Federalism's Development

Using the text and additional sources, fill in the chart by placing the following pieces of legislation, time periods, and events in chronological order with their dates, briefly describing each and stating each one's impact on developing U.S. federalism.

United States Constitution   Civil War   New Deal

McCulloch v. *Maryland*   Interstate Commerce and   Great Society
                                                  Sherman Antitrust Acts
Morrill Act   New Federalism
                                                  Sixteenth Amendment

LEGISLATION, TIME PERIOD, OR EVENT AND DATE	DESCRIPTION	IMPACT

LEGISLATION, TIME PERIOD, OR EVENT AND DATE	DESCRIPTION	IMPACT

Federalism Review

Answer the following questions.

1. What defines the limits of the authority of the national government? _____
   _____

2. Which amendment established a federal income tax? _____

3. What is federalism? _____
   _____

4. What refers to powers the Constitution withholds from the national government but not from state governments? Where in the Constitution is this directive given?
   _____

5. Define *dual federalism.* _____
   _____

6. State the "full faith and credit" clause and give its location in the Constitution.
   _____
   _____

7. What was the term for FDR's programs to help get the country out of the Great Depression?
   _____

8. Define *enumerated* or *expressed powers.* _____
   _____

9. State the "privileges and immunities" clause and give its location in the Constitution.
   _____
   _____

10. Identify the term for federal programs that grant money for specific purposes within state and local governments. _____

11. How has the focus of federalism shifted from the Constitutional Convention to today?
    _____

12. What are not spelled out in the Constitution's text but are derived from enumerated powers?
    _____

13. What is extradition, and where is it discussed in the Constitution? _____
    _____
    _____

14. What are the means of determining who gets federal aid and the amount that is to be given?
    _____

15. What is a key force in implementing national policies on the local level?

_____

16. List the requirements that are placed on the national government with regard to the states.

_____

_____

_____

_____

17. What is the elastic clause? _____

_____

_____

18. List the methods of distributing federal aid. _____

_____

19. Which type of grant was designed to streamline federal aid to states and localities?

_____

20. What is the genius of federalism and why? _____

_____

21. List the problems of federalism. _____

_____

_____

22. What is revenue sharing? _____

23. Where in the Constitution are states' responsibilities to each other and the federal govern-

ment listed? _____

24. What are the two exceptions to the "full faith and credit" clause? _____

_____

_____

25. How does America benefit from federalism? _____

_____

_____

_____

Party Functions

United States political parties have four functions: nominating candidates, governing, acting as watchdogs of the opposition, and providing a moderating influence. Choose a major U.S. party. Using various media sources, give an example of how that party illustrates each function. Include the media source or sources used for each example.

1. **Party Choice** _____

2. **Candidate Nomination**   Cite the most recent selection of candidates at the local, state, or national level. _____

   _____

   _____

   _____

3. **Governing**   Give the percent of this party's representation at the national and state levels in the House and Senate. Does this party control the presidency or state governorship?

   _____

   _____

   _____

   _____

4. **Watchdog**   Give recent comments concerning the opposition party's handling of an event, position on an issue or piece of legislation, or party members' activities.

   _____

   _____

   _____

   _____

   _____

   _____

5. **Moderating Influence**   Cite compromises within the party on legislation or a particular issue, or the handling of a party member at the local, state, or national level.

   _____

   _____

   _____

   _____

   _____

   _____

1840 Platform Resolves

With the first political party conventions came the first party platforms, formal statements of a party's position on certain issues. The following resolves are from the 1840 Democratic Platform. Read each and identify the issue being addressed and the party's position concerning that issue.

Resolve #1: Resolved, That the federal government is one of limited powers, derived solely from the constitution, and the grants of power shown therein ought to be strictly construed by all the departments and agents of the government, and that it is inexpedient and dangerous to exercise doubtful constitutional powers.

_____

_____

Resolve #2: Resolved, That the constitution does not confer upon the general government the power to commence and carry on a general system of internal improvements.

_____

_____

Resolve #3: Resolved, That the constitution does not confer authority upon the federal government, directly or indirectly, to assume the debts of the several states, contracted for local internal improvements, or other state purposes; nor would such assumption be just or expedient.

_____

_____

Resolve #5: Resolved, That it is the duty of every branch of the government to enforce and practice the most rigid economy in conducting our public affairs, and that no more revenue ought to be raised than is required to defray the necessary expenses of the government.

_____

_____

Resolve #7: Resolved, That congress has no power, under the constitution, to interfere with or control the domestic institutions of the several states, and that such states are the sole and proper judges of everything appertaining to their own affairs, not prohibited by the constitution.

_____

_____

Resolve #9: Resolved, That the liberal principles embodied by Jefferson in the Declaration of Independence, and sanctioned in the constitution, which makes ours the land of liberty, and the asylum of the oppressed of every nation, have ever been cardinal principles in the democratic faith.

_____

_____

 *Name* _____

Washington's Farewell

On September 19, 1796, after serving two presidential terms, President Washington had his farewell address published in Philadelphia's *American Daily Advertiser*. Read each excerpt and answer the questions. A dictionary would be useful for this activity.

Excerpt 1 "In contemplating the causes which may disturb our Union, it occurs as matter of serious concern that any ground should have been furnished for characterizing parties by geographical discriminations, Northern and Southern, Atlantic and Western; whence, designing men may endeavor to excite a belief that there is a real difference of local interests and views. One of the expedients of party to acquire influence within particular districts is to misrepresent the opinions and aims of other districts."

1. Give one reason for the formation of political parties. _____
_____
_____

2. How could a political party acquire influence within a particular district? _____
_____

Excerpt 2 "All obstructions to the execution of the laws, all combinations and associations, under whatever plausible character, with the real design to direct, control, or awe the regular deliberation and action of the constituted authorities, are destructive of this fundamental principle, and of fatal tendency. They serve to organize faction, to give it an artificial and extraordinary force; to put, in the place of the delegated will of the nation the will of a party, often a small but artful and enterprising minority of the community. . . ."

"However combinations or associations of the above description may now and then answer popular ends, they are likely, in the course of time and things, to become potent engines, by which cunning, ambitious, and unprincipled men will be enabled to subvert the power of the people and to usurp for themselves the reins of government, destroying afterwards the very engines which have lifted them to unjust dominion."

1. What is destructive to the execution of the laws? _____
_____
_____

2. What could take the place of the will of the nation? _____
_____

3. How does Washington describe the possible "popular ends" of these "combinations or associations" which are political parties? _____
_____
_____

Excerpt 3 "I have already intimated to you the danger of parties in the State, with particular reference to the founding of them on geographical discriminations. Let me now

43

take a more comprehensive view, and warn you in the most solemn manner against the baneful effects of the spirit of party generally."

"This spirit, unfortunately, is inseparable from our nature, having its root in the strongest passions of the human mind. It exists under different shapes in all governments, more or less stifled, controlled, or repressed; but, in those of popular form, it is seen in its greatest rankness, and is truly their worst enemy."

"The alternate domination of one faction over another, sharpened by the spirit of revenge, natural to party dissension, which in different ages and countries has perpetrated the most horrid enormities, is itself a frightful despotism. But this leads at length to a more formal and permanent despotism. The disorders and miseries which result gradually incline the minds of men to seek security and repose in the absolute power of an individual; and sooner or later the chief of some prevailing faction, more able or more fortunate than his competitors, turns this disposition to the purposes of his own elevation, on the ruins of public liberty."

1. What does *baneful* mean? _____

2. How is the "spirit" of the party described? _____

   _____

   _____

3. What is the result of a party's alternating dominance? _____

   _____

   _____

   _____

   _____

Excerpt 4 "There is an opinion that parties in free countries are useful checks upon the administration of the government and serve to keep alive the spirit of liberty. This within certain limits is probably true. . . . From their natural tendency, it is certain there will always be enough of that spirit for every salutary purpose. And there being constant danger of excess, the effort ought to be by force of public opinion, to mitigate and assuage it. . . ."

1. How do free countries look at political parties? _____

   _____

   _____

2. Define *mitigate* and *assuage*. _____

   _____

3. What effects should public opinion have on the spirit of political parties? _____

   _____

For Class Discussion: Was Washington correct in his assumptions about political parties? Support your answer.

Party Organization

Choose a major United States political party. Using additional resources, answer the following questions.

National Party Organization

1. Which party do you choose? _____

2. Who is the national party chairman? _____

3. List the national party committees and organizations. _____

_____

_____

_____

4. Where and when did the party hold its most recent national convention? _____

_____

5. What are the national party's top five issues? _____

_____

_____

_____

6. Which House and Senate members identify with your party? _____

_____

_____

State and Local Party Organization

1. Who chairs the state party organization? _____

2. List the state House and Senate members from your district that identify with your party.

_____

_____

_____

3. Who chairs your county's party organization? _____

4. List the name and office of the county-elected officials that identify with your party.

_____

_____

_____

5. Are there party organizations in the city or town in your area of residence? If so, list them and their monthly meeting dates and times. _____

_____

Term Review

Identify the term that each phrase defines.

_____ 1. Strong devotion to a political party

_____ 2. The largest number of votes cast for a candidate

_____ 3. A temporary alliance of several groups

_____ 4. Political party representatives to the party convention

_____ 5. Smallest units of election districts and party administration

_____ 6. Voting for candidates of different parties for different offices

_____ 7. A group that advances certain political goals and gains power by winning elections

_____ 8. To name candidates for public office

_____ 9. Two major parties working together to support an issue

_____ 10. The practice of giving jobs to friends and supporters

_____ 11. An election prior to the general election in which voters select the candidate who will run on each party's ticket

_____ 12. Units into which cities are often divided for city council elections

_____ 13. Groups formed around a particular issue or agenda

_____ 14. Voters who have no party affiliation

_____ 15. Formal statement of a party's position on current issues

_____ 16. Legislative districts from which only one representative is chosen

Becoming a Candidate

You want to become a candidate from your district seeking a state House of Representatives seat. Complete the following.

1. Candidate requirements _____

   _____

   _____

   _____

2. Papers that have to be filed, date to be filed, required fees, and location of filing

   _____

   _____

   _____

   _____

   _____

3. Write a press statement announcing your candidacy. _____

   _____

   _____

   _____

   _____

   _____

4. Write a brief biography about yourself. _____

   _____

   _____

   _____

   _____

5. List three issues important to your district and your position on these issues.

   _____

   _____

   _____

   _____

   _____

Campaign Tools

Choose one of the following tools for your campaign—create a bumper sticker, design an Internet website, or write a radio spot.

 *Name* _____

Chapter 9   Activity 3

State Election Laws
Answer the following questions concerning your state's election laws.

1. What are the voter qualifications? _____

   _____

   _____

2. When are the voter registration deadlines? _____

3. What are the absentee ballot deadlines? _____

4. When are absentee ballots counted? _____

5. What are the provisions for making polling places accessible to the elderly and handicapped?

   _____

   _____

6. What election day workers are to be at the polling places; what are their minimum qualifica-

   tions; and what is their pay? _____

   _____

   _____

7. What are the requirements for student workers? _____

   _____

8. When may a post-election recount be requested? _____

   _____

   _____

9. What are the recount provisions? _____

   _____

   _____

10. When do county and state ballot certifications occur? _____

    _____

    _____

Statewide Voting

Locate a map of your state with only the state and counties outlined. Using the most recent presidential or gubernatorial election numbers, color each county RED if a majority of Republicans voted or BLUE if there was a Democratic majority. Then on the map, outline the congressional districts and give their numbers. Answer the following questions.

1. Is your county more Democratic or Republican? _____

2. What is the number of the congressional district in which you live? _____

3. Does your congressional district lean more toward the Republicans or Democrats?

   _____

4. Label the three largest cities in your state, including your state capital. Identify whether these cities are in Republican or Democratic counties. _____

   _____

   _____

Do You Remember?

Answer the following.

1. What is a preliminary election held to select candidates and/or delegates to party conventions?

   _____

2. This occurs when a strong candidate on the ballot helps attract voters to other candidates on the ballot from the same party. _____

3. Who are individuals appointed by political parties and candidates to observe the polls on election day? _____

4. What are voters called who are unable to vote at their polling place on election day?

   _____

5. What is soft money? _____

   _____

   _____

6. Who is an incumbent? _____

7. This occurs when one desirous of running for a particular office announces his intention of running. _____

8. A primary in which every voter receives a ballot listing all party candidates for nomination and selects one candidate for each office. _____

9. Who are constituents? _____

10. What are paid advertisements used by state and local candidates? _____

11. What is to officially enroll for the purpose of voting? _____

12. What are expenses by a person or group that communicates to the voters to help elect or defeat a candidate without the candidate's knowledge or support? _____

13. Define *nomination*. _____

14. What is a primary called in which voters do not have to declare their party membership?

   _____

15. What is voting for all the candidates in one party? _____

16. What is the term for a location in a specific precinct where residents of that area go to vote?

   _____

17. What are PACs? _____

   _____

18. What is a formal document signed by a specific number of qualified voters for a candidate in an election district? _____

19. Define *closed primary*. _____

_____

20. What is an election used to fill an elective office called? _____

21. In which court case did the U.S. Supreme Court rule that the First Amendment was violated
by restricting a candidate's spending of his own money for campaign purposes?

_____

22. List the methods of nominating a candidate.

_____

_____

_____

_____

_____

23. What does not cost a campaign any money and aids in name recognition for an unknown

candidate? _____

24. Which amendment allowed senators to be directly elected by the people? _____

25. What is the important first step toward being elected to office? _____

_____

26. When are general elections held? _____

27. What are "Australian ballots"? _____

_____

28. What is the latest tool to aid the candidate's campaign? _____

Today's Opinions

Identify two major domestic policy issues and two foreign policy issues that America is facing. Briefly give the conservative and liberal opinions on these issues and state the biblical position.

ISSUE	CONSERVATIVE VIEW	LIBERAL VIEW	BIBLICAL VIEW
(Domestic)			
(Domestic)			
(Foreign)			
(Foreign)			

Opinions About Public Opinion

Read the following quotations concerning public opinion from Presidents Jefferson and Buchanan. What does each one say about public opinion? Do these observations hold true today? Support your answer.

Thomas Jefferson to Chevalier de Ouis, 1814

"An enlightened people, and an energetic **public opinion** . . . will control and enchain the aristocratic spirit of the government."

_____

_____

_____

_____

_____

_____

Thomas Jefferson to Lafayette, 1823

"The only security of all is in a free press. The force of **public opinion** cannot be resisted when permitted freely to be expressed. The agitation it produces must be submitted to. It is necessary, to keep the waters pure."

_____

_____

_____

_____

_____

_____

James Buchanan in a message to Congress, 1860

"Our union rests upon **public opinion**, and can never be cemented by the blood of its citizens shed in civil war."

_____

_____

_____

_____

_____

_____

Lobby Letter

An effective method of lobbying legislatures is by writing letters. Identify a state or national issue that concerns you and write a letter to a state or congressional legislator. Be specific about what you want, and if it involves a bill being voted on, identify the bill. Give an example to make the issue real and ask for a direct response on the legislator's position. See "How to Write to Public Officials" in the appendix of the American Government Student Text.

_____
_____
_____
_____
_____
_____
_____
_____
_____
_____
_____
_____
_____
_____
_____
_____
_____
_____
_____
_____
_____
_____
_____
_____
_____
_____
_____

Mass Media Cartoon

Answer the questions about the political cartoon.

SARGENT ©2003 Austin American-Statesman. Reprinted with permission of UNIVERSAL PRESS SYNDICATE. All rights reserved.

1. List the people/objects shown and what each represents. _____
   _____

2. Are there important words in the cartoon? If so, what do they indicate?
   _____
   _____
   _____

3. What issue is being presented? _____
   _____

4. What is the cartoonist communicating about this issue? What is his viewpoint?
   _____
   _____
   _____

 *Name* _____

Public Policy Review
Answer the following questions.

1. What word describes a philosophy that favors government action? _____

2. What issues are frequently included in domestic policy? _____
   _____

3. List five influences on public opinion. _____
   _____

4. Give another term for and define interest groups. _____
   _____

5. What do the words *amicus curiae* mean, and what does the phrase refer to?
   _____
   _____

6. What is C-SPAN, and what is its goal? _____
   _____
   _____
   _____
   _____

7. Define *prior restraint*. _____
   _____

8. What is the term for using various techniques to select and manipulate information so as to persuade or influence people effectively? _____

9. What word describes a philosophy that is reluctant to expand government authority?
   _____

10. What issues are included in foreign policy? _____

11. Define *opinion polls*. _____

12. List the methods used by interest groups to influence public policy. _____
    _____
    _____

13. Define *Internet*. _____
    _____

14. What gives the media and private individuals broad powers to investigate files of the federal bureaucracy? _____

15. What are the two exceptions to the media's freedom under the First Amendment?

_____

16. Define *public policy*. _____

_____

17. What word describes an individual who has a middle-of-the-road political philosophy and tends to use a pragmatic approach to political issues? _____

18. Define *agenda*. _____

19. Define and give two characteristics of *public opinion*. _____

_____

_____

_____

_____

_____

20. List ways public opinion is measured. _____

_____

21. What is the AFL-CIO? _____

22. Define *mass media*. _____

_____

23. What are surveys taken as voters leave polling places? _____

24. Which government agency can impose fines on stations for broadcasting obscene language or engaging in false advertising? _____

25. What are straw polls? _____

26. What are committees formed by special-interest groups to raise money and make contributions to specific individuals' campaigns or causes? _____

27. Define *shield laws*. _____

_____

28. What refers to published false statements that injure one's reputation? _____

29. Identify the tactic used to attempt to influence public officials in support of a group's special interest. _____

30. What is false oral communication that injures one's reputation? _____

american GOVERNMENT   *Name* _____

Chapter 11   Activity 1

Tocqueville on Legislative Powers

Read Alexis de Tocqueville's observations on the legislative powers of the United States Congress and answer the questions that follow.

The plan which had been laid down beforehand for the Constitutions of the several States was followed, in many points, in the organization of the powers of the Union. The Federal legislature of the Union was composed of a Senate and a House of Representatives. A spirit of conciliation prescribed the observance of distinct principles in the formation of these two assemblies. I have already shown that two contrary interests were opposed to each other in the establishment of the Federal Constitution. These two interests had given rise to two opinions. It was the wish of one party to convert the Union into a league of independent States, or a sort of congress, at which the representatives of the several peoples would meet to discuss certain points of their common interests. The other party desired to unite the inhabitants of the American colonies into one sole nation, and to establish a Government which should act as the sole representative of the nation, as far as the limited sphere of its authority would permit. The practical consequences of these two theories were exceedingly different.

The question was, whether a league was to be established instead of a national Government; whether the majority of the State, instead of the majority of the inhabitants of the Union, was to give the law: for every State, the small as well as the great, would then remain in the full enjoyment of its independence, and enter the Union upon a footing of perfect equality. If, however, the inhabitants of the United States were to be considered as belonging to one and the same nation, it would be just that the majority of the citizens of the Union should prescribe the law. Of course the lesser States could not subscribe to the application of this doctrine without, in fact, abdicating their existence in relation to the sovereignty of the Confederation; since they would have passed from the condition of a co-equal and co-legislative authority to that of an insignificant fraction of a great people. But if the former system would have invested them with an excessive authority, the latter would have annulled their influence altogether. Under these circumstances the result was, that the strict rules of logic were evaded, as is usually the case when interests are opposed to arguments. A middle course was hit upon by the legislators, which brought together by force two systems theoretically irreconcilable.

The principle of the independence of the States prevailed in the formation of the Senate, and that of the sovereignty of the nation predominated in the composition of the House of Representatives. It was decided that each State should send two senators to Congress, and a number of representatives proportioned to its population. It results from this arrangement that the State of New York has at the present day forty representatives and only two senators; the State of Delaware has two senators and only one representative; the State of Delaware is therefore equal to the State of New York in the Senate, whilst the latter has forty times the influence of the former in the House of Representatives. Thus, if the minority of the nation preponderates in the Senate, it may paralyze the decisions of the majority represented in the other House, which is contrary to the spirit of constitutional government.

These facts show how rare and how difficult it is rationally and logically to combine all the several parts of legislation. In the course of time different interests arise, and different principles are sanctioned by the same people; and when a general constitution is to be established, these interests and principles are so many natural obstacles to the rigorous application of any political system, with all its consequences. The early stages of national existence are the only periods at which it is possible to maintain the complete logic of legislation; and when we perceive a nation in the enjoyment of this advantage, before we hasten to conclude that it is wise, we should do well to remember that it is young. When the Federal Constitution was formed, the interests of independence for the separate States, and the interest of union for the whole people, were the only two conflicting interests which existed amongst the Anglo-Americans, and a compromise was necessarily made between them.

It is, however, just to acknowledge that this part of the Constitution has not hitherto produced those evils which might have been feared. All the States are young and contiguous; their customs, their ideas, and their exigencies are not dissimilar; and the differences which result from their size or inferiority do not suffice to set their interests at variance. The small States have consequently never been induced to league themselves together in the Senate to oppose the designs of the larger ones; and indeed there is so irresistible an authority in the legitimate expression of the will of a people that the Senate could offer but a feeble opposition to the vote of the majority of the House of Representatives.

It must not be forgotten, on the other hand, that it was not in the power of the American legislators to reduce to a single nation the people for whom they were making laws. The object of the Federal Constitution was not to destroy the independence of the States, but to restrain it. By acknowledging the real authority of these secondary communities (and it was impossible to deprive them of it), they disavowed beforehand the habitual use of constraint in enforcing the decisions of the majority. Upon this principle the introduction of the influence of the States into the mechanism of the Federal Government was by no means to be wondered at, since it only attested the existence of an acknowledged power, which was to be humored and not forcibly checked.

1. Where did Tocqueville say the plan for Congress had been laid down? _____

_____

2. What were the two opinions that opposed each other in the establishment of the federal

   Constitution? _____

   _____

   _____

3. What was the main question concerning the establishment of the federal government's

   legislative powers? _____

   _____

4. What was the solution to this main question? _____

   _____

5. Which principle prevailed in the formation of the Senate, and how was the principle implemented? _____

_____

_____

6. Which principle predominated in the composition of the House of Representatives, and how was it implemented? _____

_____

_____

7. What did Tocqueville say was "contrary to the spirit" of constitutional government?

_____

_____

_____

8. What does Tocqueville say these facts show? _____

_____

_____

9. What has changed since Tocqueville made the observation referred to in question 7?

_____

_____

10. What did Tocqueville say would happen to cause "natural obstacles" to the application of any political system? _____

_____

11. Thus, according to Tocqueville, when is the only time period in which it is possible to maintain the "complete logic of legislation"? _____

12. Give Tocqueville's reasons for the answer to the above question. _____

_____

_____

_____

_____

13. What did Tocqueville say was the object of the federal Constitution? Explain what he meant.

_____

_____

_____

_____

Bonus Discussion: Using other resources explain briefly who Alexis de Tocqueville was and why he was in the United States in the 1830s.

_____

_____

_____

_____

_____

_____

_____

_____

_____

_____

_____

_____

Which Committees?

Using other resources, identify your state's two senators and the House member from your congressional district. List the committees on which each serves. Identify each committee as a standing or joint committee and identify any committees they chair with a "C".

SENATOR	SENATOR	REPRESENTATIVE
COMMITTEES	COMMITTEES	COMMITTEES

american GOVERNMENT

A Bill Becomes Law

Describe each step of a bill's journey.

Step One: Introducing a Bill _____

_____

_____

_____

Step Two: Committee Deliberation _____

_____

_____

_____

_____

Step Three: Full House Vote _____

_____

_____

_____

_____

Step Four: Conference Committee _____

_____

_____

_____

_____

Step Five: Presidential Signature _____

_____

_____

_____

_____

Congressional Structure Review

Answer the following questions.

1. What did the Great Compromise at the Constitutional Convention lead to? _____
   _____

2. Define *single-member district*. _____
   _____

3. Define *caucus*. What term do Republicans use instead? _____
   _____

4. Which position in the House of Representatives is the only position named in the
   Constitution? Who serves in this position today? _____
   _____

5. Define *term limits*. _____
   _____

6. List the different types of committees in Congress. _____
   _____

7. What is the motion to stop debate called? _____

8. Define *gerrymandering* and explain how it got this name. _____
   _____
   _____
   _____
   _____

9. Which position in the Senate is mainly an honorary position given to the most senior member of the Senate's majority party? Who serves in this position today? _____
   _____

10. What is the franking privilege, and who uses it? _____
    _____

11. Which type of congressional committee is permanent, is composed of House and Senate
    members, and serves as an advisory board to other congressional committees?
    _____

12. Define *pocket veto*. _____
    _____

13. What is an official count of a country's population? _____

14. Who in the House and Senate is the leader of the party with the most members? Who serves in this position in the House and in the Senate today? _____

_____

15. What do critics call unnecessary trips taken by members of Congress? _____

16. Which type of congressional committee is temporary and is drawn from both chambers to work out a compromise agreement on a bill? _____

17. What is a filibuster, and which house of Congress uses it? _____

_____

18. What is the term for a geographical area in a state represented by a House member?

_____

19. Which amendment changed the method of the election of senators? Explain the change.

_____

_____

20. Who in the House and Senate is the leader of the party with the second most members? Who serves in this position in the House and in the Senate today? _____

_____

21. Which type of congressional committee is permanent and is more powerful than other types of committees? _____

22. Within congressional committees, who has significant powers? _____

23. Define *reapportionment*. _____

_____

24. What is a coalition? _____

25. Who are the assistant majority/minority congressional leaders, and what are their responsibilities? Who are these majority/minority congressional leaders in the House and Senate today?

_____

_____

_____

_____

 american **GOVERNMENT**   *Name* _____

War Powers Resolution
Read the following sections from the War Powers Resolution. Answer the questions.

Purpose and Policy

Section 2. (a) It is the purpose of this joint resolution to fulfill the intent of the framers of the Constitution of the United States and insure that the collective judgement of both the Congress and the President will apply to the introduction of the United States Armed Forces into hostilities, or into situations where imminent involvement in hostilities is clearly indicated by the circumstances, and to the continued use of such forces in hostilities or in such situations.

(b) Under Article I, Section 8, of the Constitution, it is specifically provided that the Congress shall have the power to make all laws necessary and proper for carrying into execution, not only its own powers but also all other powers vested by the Constitution in the Government of the United States, or in any department or officer thereof.

(c) The constitutional powers of the President as Commander-in-Chief to introduce United States Armed Forces into hostilities, or into situations where imminent involvement in hostilities is clearly indicated by the circumstances, are exercised only pursuant to (1) a declaration of war, (2) specific statutory authorization, or (3) a national emergency created by attack upon the United States, its territories or possessions, or its armed forces.

Consultation

Section 3. The President in every possible instance shall consult with Congress before introducing United States Armed Forces into hostilities or into situation where imminent involvement in hostilities is clearly indicated by the circumstances, and after every such introduction shall consult regularly with the Congress until United States Armed Forces are no longer engaged in hostilities or have been removed from such situations.

1. What is the purpose of the War Powers Resolution? _____
   _____
   _____

2. What is the War Powers Resolution to insure? _____
   _____
   _____

3. Where in the Constitution is power given to Congress to make and carry out the necessary laws pertaining to the United States government or any department or officer of the government? _____
   _____

4. List the instances in which the president may send United States Armed Forces into hostilities or situations where hostilities may occur. _____

_____

_____

_____

5. What does the president have to do prior to committing United States forces into hostilities?

_____

6. After United States Armed Forces are committed, what is the responsibility of the president?

_____

_____

_____

Discussion: What is the most recent implementation of the War Powers Resolution? What prompted its use? What did the president request, and how did Congress respond?

_____

_____

_____

_____

_____

_____

_____

_____

_____

_____

_____

_____

_____

_____

_____

_____

_____

Design a Stamp

Design a postal stamp.

Pork Political Cartoon

Read the cartoon and answer the questions.

Copyright, 2004, Tribune Media Services. Reprinted with permission.

1. List the people/objects and what each represents. _____

   _____

   _____

   _____

2. Are there important words in the cartoon? If so, what do they indicate? _____

   _____

3. What issue is being addressed? _____

   _____

4. What is the cartoonist communicating about this issue? What is his viewpoint?

   _____

   _____

   _____

Reviewing Congressional Powers

Answer the following questions.

1. Which amendment allowed Congress to tax without regard to population? _____

   _____

2. List and define the two technical matters related to military action in Article I, Section 8, Clause 11 of the Constitution. _____

   _____

   _____

   _____

3. Define *implied powers.* _____

   _____

4. What is impeachment? _____

   _____

   _____

5. What are government compensation programs that Congress has protected by law?

   _____

6. What is the practice in which a member of Congress supports a colleague's spending project in return for support for his own pork-barrel legislation? _____

7. What are enumerated powers? _____

   _____

8. Define *interstate commerce.* _____

9. What limits a president's power to use the military in a conflict? _____

10. How did the framers of the Constitution show their interest in protecting capitalism?

    _____

    _____

11. Which clause is the basis for the extraordinary powers of Congress and the federal government in general? _____

12. Define *subpoena.* _____

    _____

13. Where is the provision in the Constitution for the election of a vice president if a vacancy occurs? _____

14. Which constitutional powers are not withheld from the states, but are withheld from the national government? _____

15. What is pork-barrel politics? _____

_____

16. What is a tax on an import called? _____

17. Explain Hamilton's meaning of "general welfare." _____

_____

_____

18. What is the single greatest authority given to our national government? _____

19. What are taxes on the production, sale, or use of items and taxes on certain business practices?

_____

20. Define *citizenship*. _____

_____

21. Which piece of legislation established the provision for a chief justice, associate justices, circuit courts, and federal district courts? _____

22. What are the Senate proceedings that some government appointees have to go through to be approved for their positions? _____

23. List the House and Senate's nonlegislative powers and identify which house of Congress has each. _____

_____

_____

_____

_____

_____

24. Identify the formal approval process of a constitution, constitutional amendment, or treaty.

_____

american GOVERNMENT

Name _____

National Convention Cartoon

Read the political cartoon and answer the questions.

Mallard Fillmore . . . by Bruce Tinsley (Week of July 31, 2000)

©Reprinted with special Permission of King Features Syndicate.

1. For each frame, list the people/objects and what each represents. _____

   _____

   _____

   _____

   _____

2. Are there important words? If so, what do they represent? _____

   _____

   _____

   _____

   _____

   _____

3. What issue is being addressed? _____

   _____

4. What is the cartoonist communicating about this issue? What is his viewpoint?

   _____

   _____

   _____

   _____

   _____

Undecided Voter Cartoon

Read the political cartoon and answer the questions.

Mallard Fillmore . . . by Bruce Tinsley (Week of September 25, 2000)

©*Reprinted with special Permission of King Features Syndicate.*

1. For each frame, list the people/objects and what each represents. _____

   _____

   _____

2. Are there important words? If so, what do they indicate? _____

   _____

   _____

   _____

   _____

   _____

   _____

3. What issue is being addressed? _____

   _____

4. What is the cartoonist communicating about this issue? What is his viewpoint?

   _____

   _____

   _____

   _____

   _____

Electoral College

Label each state. Identify the number of electoral votes each state gets. According to the most recent presidential election, color those states BLUE whose electoral votes went to the DEMOCRATIC candidate, RED whose electoral votes went to the REPUBLICAN candidate, and YELLOW whose electoral votes went to a third party.

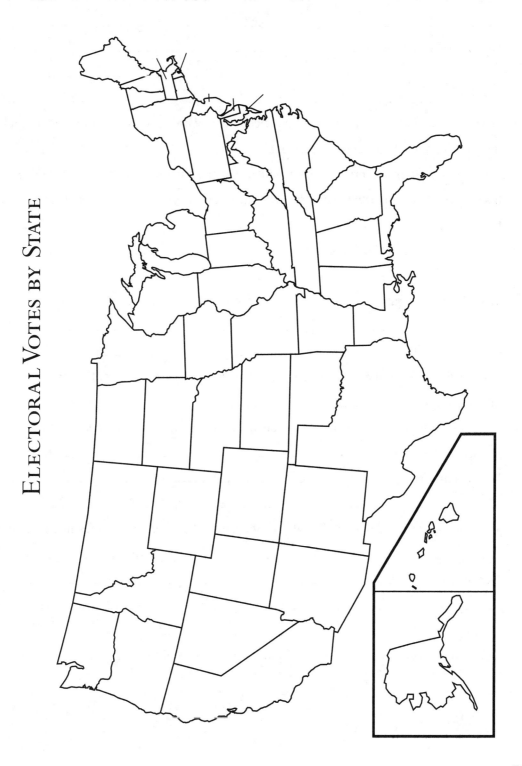

ELECTORAL VOTES BY STATE

Chapter Review

Answer the following questions.

1. What are the two basic purposes of the presidential primary? _____

    _____

    _____

2. Define *crossover voting.* _____

    _____

    _____

3. What is the term for party leaders and officeholders who serve as uncommitted delegates to the party's national convention? _____

4. What phrase refers to a presidential candidate's choosing a running mate who can strengthen his chance of being elected due to specific ideology, geography, race, gender, or other characteristics? _____

5. When is the general election held? _____

    _____

6. Why is the electoral college considered a safeguard? _____

    _____

    _____

7. What is the term for the president's release of a convicted person from the remainder of his or her sentence? _____

8. What are preliminary nominating elections that are held to select candidates and/or delegates to party conventions? _____

9. Define *party platform.* _____

    _____

10. What is a speech made on the first day of the national convention by a leading party member? _____

    _____

11. Define *brokered convention.* _____

    _____

    _____

12. What do the media use to try to predict an election's outcome? _____

 *Name* _____

Chapter 14   Activity 1

President vs. King

In *Federalist No. 69,* Alexander Hamilton compares the office of the president of the United States with that of the king of Great Britain. Read the following excerpt and identify the differences between the two.

The President of the United States would be an officer elected by the people for FOUR years; the king of Great Britain is a perpetual and HEREDITARY prince. The one would be amenable to personal punishment and disgrace; the person of the other is sacred and inviolable. The one would have a QUALIFIED negative upon the acts of the legislative body; the other has an ABSOLUTE negative. The one would have a right to command the military and naval forces of the nation; the other, in addition to this right, possesses that of DECLARING war, and of RAISING and REGULATING fleets and armies by his own authority. The one would have a concurrent power with a branch of the legislature in the formation of treaties; the other is the SOLE POSSES-SOR of the power of making treaties. The one would have a like concurrent authority in appointing to offices; the other is the sole author of all appointments. The one can confer no privileges whatever; the other can make denizens of aliens, noblemen of commoners; can erect corporations with all the rights incident to corporate bodies. The one can prescribe no rules concerning the commerce or currency of the nation; the other is in several respects the arbiter of commerce, and in this capacity can estab-lish markets and fairs, can regulate weights and measures, can lay embargoes for a limited time, can coin money, can authorize or prohibit the circulation of foreign coin. The one has no particle of spiritual jurisdiction; the other is the supreme head and governor of the national church! What answer shall we give to those who would per-suade us that things so unlike resemble each other? The same that ought to be given to those who tell us that a government, the whole power of which would be in the hands of the elective and periodical servants of the people, is an aristocracy, a monarchy, and a despotism.

CHARACTERISTICS	PRESIDENT	KING
1. Origin of leadership		
2. Length of service		
3. Accountability		

CHARACTERISTICS	PRESIDENT	KING
4. Veto power		
5. Command of military and naval forces		
6. Raising and regulating military and naval forces		
7. Declaring war		
8. Making treaties		
9. Making office appointments		
10. Conferring privileges		
11. Make laws concerning commerce or currency		
12. Spiritual jurisdiction		

Comparing Presidents

Choose a president from each of the following time periods. Using additional resources, complete the chart with the appropriate information and answer the discussion question.

	1789–1860	1861–1945	1945–Present
President			
Date and Place of Birth			
Education			
Occupation Prior to Presidency			
Major Domestic Policy Issues			
Major Foreign Policy Issues			

Discussion: Of these three presidents, who do you think was the most successful in his domestic policies and why?

_____

_____

_____

_____

_____

_____

_____

Comparing First Ladies

Choose a First Lady from each of the following time periods. Using additional resources, complete the chart with the appropriate information and answer the discussion question.

	1789–1860	1861–1945	1945–Present
First Lady			
Date and Place of Birth			
Education			
Marriage Date and Number of Children			
Personality Description			
Contributions and/or Interests as First Lady			

Discussion: Of these three First Ladies, who do you think made the most positive contribution to the position of First Lady and why?

_____

_____

_____

_____

_____

_____

_____

Biblical Leadership

Read each passage, identify the quality or qualities of biblical leadership in each passage, and answer the discussion questions.

1. Romans 13:1–4 _____
   _____
   _____
   _____

2. Matthew 23:11 _____
   _____

3. Colossians 3:23 _____
   _____
   _____

4. Isaiah 1:17 _____
   _____

5. Jeremiah 29:7 _____
   _____
   _____

Discussion

1. Do any United States presidents illustrate one or more of these qualities? If so, identify the president, identify the quality or qualities, and explain your answer.

   _____
   _____
   _____
   _____
   _____
   _____

2. Do any United States presidents illustrate the opposite of these biblical qualities? If so, identify the president and explain your answer.

   _____
   _____
   _____
   _____
   _____

Presidential Review

Answer the following questions.

1. Define *executive agreement*? Does Congress have any power over executive agreements?

    _____

    _____

    _____

2. How does the president use his State of the Union speech? _____

    _____

    _____

3. Define *tenure* and identify where it is mentioned in the Constitution. _____

    _____

4. What are executive orders? _____

5. What is the purpose of the Twenty-fifth Amendment? _____

    _____

    _____

6. Who are the individuals responsible to the president for the departments that they head?

    _____

7. What are covert operations? _____

8. Which amendment restricts the president to two terms? _____

9. What is impeachment, and which presidents have been impeached? _____

    _____

    _____

10. What probably exerts more influence on the president's policies and his legislative programs

    than any other segment of the executive branch? _____

    _____

11. If the president opposes a bill passed by Congress, what does he do? _____

    _____

12. When is the president considered a lame duck? _____

    _____

    _____

The Cabinet

Identify the head of each cabinet department. Choose one department head and, on the back of this page, give a brief biographical sketch.

Department of State

_____

Department of the Treasury

_____

Department of Defense

_____

Department of Justice

_____

Department of the Interior

_____

Department of Agriculture

_____

Department of Commerce

_____

Department of Labor

_____

Department of Health and Human Services

_____

Department of Housing and Urban Development

_____

Department of Transportation

_____

Department of Energy

_____

Department of Education

_____

Department of Veterans Affairs

_____

Department of Homeland Security

_____

Biographical Sketch

_____
_____
_____
_____
_____
_____
_____
_____
_____
_____
_____
_____
_____
_____
_____
_____
_____
_____
_____
_____
_____
_____
_____

Bible Bureaucratic Positions

David and Solomon had individuals in their governments who advised them and helped them carry out executive responsibilities. Read the Scripture passages. Identify the individuals, the positions, and (using a Bible commentary or Bible dictionary) give a brief description of those positions. Also, identify any corresponding bureaucratic positions in the United States executive branch.

David's Government

1. II Samuel 8:15–18 _____

_____

_____

_____

_____

_____

_____

_____

_____

_____

_____

_____

_____

2. II Samuel 20:24 _____

_____

_____

_____

Solomon's Government

I Kings 4:1–6 _____

_____

_____

_____

_____

_____

Bureaucracy Cartoon

Draw a political cartoon focusing on the size of government or the bureaucratic problems of red tape, duplication, or waste. On the back of this page explain your cartoon.

Cartoon Explanation

_____

_____

_____

_____

_____

_____

_____

_____

_____

_____

_____

_____

_____

_____

_____

_____

_____

_____

_____

_____

_____

_____

Bureaucracy Review

Answer the following questions.

1. What event illuminated the federal government's administrative weaknesses and prompted the hiring of many new officials? _____

2. Who advises the president on issues of politics, policy, and management? _____
   _____

3. Define *cabinet*. _____
   _____

4. What is statutory law? _____

5. What is the federal bureaucracy sometimes called? _____

6. What provided citizens access to information previously withheld? _____
   _____

7. List the six major bureaucratic problems. _____
   _____

8. Identify the principle of delegation. _____
   _____

9. What is the civil service? _____
   _____

10. Who is the official spokesperson for an administration? _____

11. What reflects the growth of the country and government involvement in social issues?
    _____
    _____

12. Define *administrative law*. _____

13. How does Congress exercise checks over the bureaucracy? _____
    _____
    _____

14. What is the mismanagement of money, time, and personnel by the government?
    _____

15. Define *bureaucrat*. _____
    _____

16. What act established the Civil Service Commission and abolished the spoils system?
    _____

17. Which agency is the president's policymaking group over security and intelligence matters?

    _____

18. Who are known as clients? _____

    _____

19. What is the process of examining a department's compliance with the law and scrutinizing its

    budget requests? _____

20. What is red tape? _____

21. Define *bureaucratese*. _____

    _____

22. List the four distinctive characteristics of the U.S. bureaucracy.

    _____

    _____

    _____

    _____

    _____

23. Define *bureaucracy*. _____

    _____

    _____

24. What was the new standard for hiring and promoting civil employees that was established

    by the 1883 Pendleton Act? _____

25. What are SOPs? _____

    _____

 american|**GOVERNMENT** *Name* _____

Chapter 16   Activity 1

Goal Achievement

Give an example of how the United States is presently seeking to achieve each of its foreign policy goals.

GOAL	EXAMPLE
National Security	
Alliance Security	
International Stability	
Economic Development	

© 2004 BJU Press. Reproduction prohibited.

91

Foreign Policy Development

For each time period, list events that helped develop United States foreign policy. Identify the foreign policy goal(s) (National Security, Alliance Security, International Stability, Economic Development) associated with each event.

TIME PERIOD	EVENTS AND GOALS
1790–1890	
1890–1910	
1910–40	
1940–91	
1991 to the present	

Who's Who at the UN

Using additional resources, answer the following questions concerning the United Nations.

1. Who is the current secretary-general, and which country is he from? _____
   _____

2. How many countries are in the General Assembly? _____
   _____
   _____

3. Who are the five permanent Security Council members? Which fifteen member nations are
   serving on the Security Council with the five permanent members? _____
   _____
   _____
   _____

4. What are the five geographical groups that make up the Economic and Social Council? List
   one member state from each group.
   _____
   _____
   _____
   _____
   _____

5. Which fifteen countries have a judge serving on the International Court of Justice? Does the
   United States have a judge on the court? _____
   _____
   _____
   _____
   _____

Foreign Policy Methods

The United States has used various methods to achieve its foreign policy goals. Give a historical example (before 2000) and a current example of each method.

METHOD	HISTORICAL EXAMPLE	CURRENT EXAMPLE
Diplomacy		
Treaties and Multinational Organizations		
Foreign Aid		
Sanctions		
Military Action and Espionage		

Foreign Policy Review

Answer the following.

1. What supplied billions of dollars to Western Europe to rebuild shattered economics and bolster democracy? _____

2. What is nuclear deterrence? _____

_____

_____

3. What is meant by "cultural imperialism"? _____

_____

4. Define *consulate*. _____

_____

5. Which department is the largest segment of the national government? _____

6. Where in the Constitution is treaty ratification stated, and what is required? _____

_____

7. Identify the trade agreement that calls for free trade to be gradually implemented between the United States, Canada, and Mexico. _____

8. Define *sanctions*. _____

_____

9. What is the use of unlawful means of war to achieve one's goals? _____

10. Define *rogue nation*. _____

_____

_____

11. List examples of weapons of mass destruction. _____

_____

12. Define *foreign policy*. _____

_____

13. How may allied nations gain support? _____

_____

14. What was the dominant theme of America's foreign policy during its first century, and which administration formulated it? _____

15. Define *containment*. When did the U.S. use containment as a part of its foreign policy?

_____

_____

16. Which two U.S. departments administer international relations and national security?

_____

17. Define *embassies*. What type of officials head them, and how are they placed in these positions?

_____

_____

_____

18. What is the Pentagon? Where is it located, and who works there? _____

_____

_____

_____

19. What are formal agreements made between nations or groups of nations? _____

20. Define *fourth-generation warfare*. _____

_____

Identify the following divisions of the United Nations.

1. Main judicial body dealing with international law _____

2. Primary representative body _____

3. Promotes fundamental human rights as defined by the UN _____

4. Acts as the main administrative body _____

5. Deals with peace and security issues _____

Identify what each of the following abbreviations represents and briefly state the organization's purpose.

1. NSC _____

_____

2. CIA _____

_____

3. EU _____

_____

4. WTO _____

_____

5. NATO _____

_____

The Law of the Lord

Read each verse, give the meaning, and explain how each verse applies to you.

Psalm 19:7—The law of the Lord is perfect, converting the soul: the testimony of the Lord is sure, making wise the simple.

Meaning:

_____

_____

_____

_____

_____

Application:

_____

_____

_____

_____

_____

Psalm 37:31—The law of his God is in his heart; none of his steps shall slide.

Meaning:

_____

_____

_____

_____

_____

Application:

_____

_____

_____

_____

_____

Psalm 119:165—Great peace have they which love thy law: and nothing shall offend them.

Meaning:

_____

_____

_____

_____

_____

Application:

_____

_____

_____

_____

_____

Proverbs 6:23—For the commandment is a lamp; and the law is light.

Meaning:

_____

_____

_____

_____

_____

Application:

_____

_____

_____

_____

_____

Name _____

Supreme Court Political Cartoon
Read the political cartoon and answer the questions.

"By permission of Chip Bok and Creators Syndicate, Inc"

1. For each frame, list the people/objects and what each represents. _____

    _____

    _____

2. Are there important words or numbers in the cartoon? If so, what do they indicate?

    _____

    _____

    _____

    _____

3. What issue is being addressed? _____

    _____

    _____

4. What is the cartoonist communicating about this issue, and what is his viewpoint?

    _____

    _____

    _____

    _____

    _____

american|GOVERNMENT

Chapter 17   Activity 3

Supreme Court Justice

Choose a current United States Supreme Court justice and answer the following questions.

1. What is the name of the chosen justice? _____

2. What is the date and place of his or her birth? _____
_____

3. Is the justice married? If so, to whom, and does he or she have children? _____
_____

4. What colleges/universities did the justice attend, and what degrees were earned?
_____
_____

5. What positions did the justice hold prior to taking a seat on the Court? _____
_____
_____

6. Which president nominated the justice, and when did he or she take a seat on the Court?
_____
_____

7. Which circuit/circuits are allotted to this justice, and what areas in the United States are included? _____
_____

8. What was the most recent case the justice heard, and how did he or she rule? _____
_____
_____
_____
_____

© 2004 BJU Press. Reproduction prohibited.

Reviewing the Judiciary

Answer the following questions.

1. Define *precedents*. _____

2. What is the revelation of God's law through the Scriptures? _____

3. Which part of the Constitution allows the president to appoint all federal judges with Senate approval? _____

4. Define *judicial review*. _____
_____

5. Which court case made abortion legal? _____

6. What is justice? _____

7. Define *stare decisis*. _____
_____

8. What term identifies Supreme Court judges? _____

9. Identify the Roman legal materials collected and published by Roman emperor Justinian.
_____

10. What are district courts? _____
_____

11. Give the meaning of *writ of certiorari* and tell what it refers to in the U.S. judicial system.
_____
_____
_____

12. What is indicated when a chief justice writes the majority opinion? _____
_____

13. What is senatorial courtesy? _____
_____
_____

14. Through which court case did Chief Justice Marshall declare the doctrine of judicial review?
_____

15. What term describes the philosophy of those who support a broad constructionist view of constitutional interpretation? _____

16. Define *common law*. _____
_____

17. What work written by Blackstone strongly influenced America's founders? _____

18. Define *judicial federalism.* _____

19. What term refers to a court's right to be the first to hear a case before any other court considers it? _____

20. Define *natural law.* _____

21. Identify the term for a court's power to decide appeals. _____

22. Define *appeal.* _____

23. Define *dissenting opinion.* _____

24. In which case did the Marshall Court rule that state taxation of the Second Bank of the United States was unconstitutional? _____

25. What term describes the philosophy of those who support a strict constructionist view of constitutional interpretation? _____

26. Define *concurring opinion.* _____

27. What do district courts use to indict, or charge, accused criminals? _____

28. List the five basic ways state judges are chosen. _____

29. Define *supremacy clause.* _____

30. What do district courts use to decide a case's outcome? _____

Freedom of the Press

Read the excerpt from Alexis de Tocqueville's *Democracy in America*, Volume 1.
List Tocqueville's observations about the American press.

But although the press is limited to these resources, its influence in America is immense. It is the power which impels the circulation of political life through all the districts of that vast territory. Its eye is constantly open to detect the secret springs of political designs, and to summon the leaders of all parties to the bar of public opinion. It rallies the interests of the community round certain principles, and it draws up the creed which factions adopt; for it affords a means of intercourse between parties which hear, and which address each other without ever having been in immediate contact. When a great number of the organs of the press adopt the same line of conduct, their influence becomes irresistible; and public opinion, when it is perpetually assailed from the same side, eventually yields to the attack. In the United States each separate journal exercises but little authority, but the power of the periodical press is only second to that of the people.

_____

_____

_____

_____

_____

_____

_____

_____

_____

_____

_____

_____

_____

_____

For class discussion: Give an example of major news services emphasizing a specific issue and thereby influencing the public to take the view of the press.

Five Freedoms

Issues involving each of our five First Amendment freedoms continue to arise. Give a recent example for each freedom.

Freedom of Religion

_____

_____

_____

_____

Freedom of Speech

_____

_____

_____

_____

Freedom of the Press

_____

_____

_____

_____

Freedom of Assembly

_____

_____

_____

_____

Freedom of Petition

_____

_____

_____

_____

american|GOVERNMENT

Name _____

Right to Bear Arms Cartoon
Read the political cartoon and answer the questions.

Clay Bennett© The Christian Science Monitor

1. List the people/objects and what each represents. _____
   _____
   _____

2. Are there important words in the cartoon? If so, what do they indicate?
   _____
   _____
   _____
   _____

3. What issue is being addressed? _____
   _____

4. What is the cartoonist communicating about the issue? What is his viewpoint?
   _____
   _____
   _____
   _____
   _____

Voting Rights Cartoon

Read the political cartoon and answer the questions.

Jericho, U.S.A.

---from The Herblock Gallery (Simon & Schuster, 1968)

1. List the people/objects and what each represents. _____

_____

_____

2. Are there important words or numbers? If so, what do they indicate? _____

_____

_____

_____

_____

3. What issue is being addressed? _____

4. What is the cartoonist communicating about the issue? What is his viewpoint? _____

_____

_____

_____

_____

_____

Reviewing Rights and Responsibilities

Answer the following questions.

1. In which case did the Supreme Court forbid teacher-led prayers in public schools? _____
   _____

2. Define *subversion.* _____
   _____

3. What is the expression of ideas through actions instead of words? _____

4. Define *substantive due process.* _____
   _____

5. Identify the term for being tried twice for the same crime in the same court. _____
   _____

6. What are civil rights? _____
   _____

7. Identify the term for a person's making admissions in a criminal case that could be used
   against him in court. _____

8. Which amendment guarantees the right to jury trials for civil cases between citizens involving disputes exceeding twenty dollars? _____

9. Identify the term for money paid in order to vote and the amendment that ended this practice
   in federal elections. _____

10. List the two parts of the First Amendment's freedom of religion declaration. _____
    _____

11. Which act made it illegal to advocate the violent overthrow of the government, to teach others
    to take such actions, or to be a member of an organization that conspires to overthrow the
    government? _____

12. Which freedom is not mentioned in the Constitution but has been inferred from the right of
    free speech and right of petition? _____

13. Which amendment protects citizens from unreasonable searches and seizures? _____
    _____

14. Define *capital punishment.* _____

15. In which court case did the Supreme Court declare all segregated school facilities to be in
    violation of the Fourteenth Amendment? _____
    _____

16. What was the intention of the First Amendment establishment clause? _____

_____

_____

17. Define *sedition*. _____

_____

18. What is the term for the list that the police must recite to the accused prior to questioning?

_____

19. What will the courts grant to the defendant if the authorities do not try him for a crime or

release him? _____

20. Which act established no discrimination at any hotel, cafeteria, gas station, or theater and

created the Equal Employment Opportunity Commission? _____

_____

21. What is the term for protecting individual freedoms from government intrusion? _____

_____

22. What is the difference between slander and libel? _____

_____

23. List American civil rights.

_____

_____

_____

24. Which amendment gives the right to bear arms? _____

25. What are *ex post facto* laws? _____

_____

_____

26. List American civil liberties.

_____

_____

_____

27. Which amendment provides important protections for the accused? _____

28. What is the goal of the new civil rights groups of today? _____

_____